To Sandy! Thank you for your support. Please enjoy!

In Venice I Could Sing

Patricia Martin

Patricia

In Venice I Could Sing

Copyright © 2021 by Patricia Martin

www.localgemspoetrypress.com

Dedicated to Ogostino Mancini, the musician who got me out of the writing closet and performing in public; Saul Bennett and Donald Lev, the venerable Woodstock poets who took me under their wing; the many poets and writers I have had the privilege of listening to and sharing with; James P. Wagner for supporting my work; and Jack! Jack! Jack!

Foreword

By Jack Sheedy

Patricia Martin has poetry in her soul. When I met her in 2017, she was reading her poetry at an open mic, an event I attended in order to read from my memoir, *Sting of the Heat Bug* (Signalman Publishing, 2012). The very next night, by chance, we met again, this time at a monthly poetry open mic event called SpeakEasy, which she created and hosted. And days later, again by chance, we met at a staged reading of poetry. (We had both come stag so we sat together, which is a poem in itself.)

Poetry flows through this woman. You will see this in such personal poems as "The Walk" and "Secrets Weigh," foreshadowing the #MeToo Movement in their frank, stark depiction of sexual violation. You will see it in the longing-for-love poems like "How Do I Trust the Heart Again" and "Tossing Petals." And you will rejoice at it while reading "In Venice I Could Sing" and "What Is Sweet, What Is Good."

A poet is a person with feelings that simply overflow her being, so that they bubble up in the form of words that arouse feelings in other people. One of the most powerful poems in this collection is "Blood and Ink: Soldiers' Letters Home from War," a poem comprised of verbatim excerpts from letters soldiers sent home to loved ones from different wars, different times. Martin's editorial skill —"what to leave in, what to leave out," as Bob Seger sings—and weaving them together is what makes this astonishing poem such an emotional cry for peace. I challenge anyone to read it without tissues.

You've heard enough from me. Now put aside some time for Patricia Martin. Find a comfortable chair, a quiet moment, an hour or two to yourself to absorb these poems. You will not be the same person afterwards.

Jack Sheedy is a poet, a playwright and an award-winning journalist living in northwest Connecticut. His latest book is an essay collection, Magical Acts in Two Suitcases *(2020), available on Amazon or from* <u>www.jacksheedy.com</u>.

Table of Contents

These Things You Did Not Ask of Me

To hurl myself out of the shower
sheathed in soap
and grab the phone call that might be you
but wasn't

To say "maybe" to plans offered by others
holding the door open for you to come first
if you came at all

To have you always in the back of my mind
clamoring for attention,
or have my stomach turn inside out
with fear you may be gone without a word

To not take another lover
like the darkly handsome poet who had just lost his cat
and could have found comfort in my arms

All these things and more you never asked of me, did you?

But you did ask me to want nothing, and give nothing

Except laugh at the lunatic pink temple moon
read the wise words of great mystics
walk silently along the lake in tandem with the wind

1

then lay me down on soft moss under pine boughs and
breathe you in

You asked me not to call your house
because your estranged wife would make your home hours
unbearable
and you simply could not have that

You asked me not to put my heart in your hands
you could not bear the burden
although of course by then it was too late

How Do I Trust the Heart Again?

It has turned on me
in a most unexpected way
one that sent me strapped into an ambulance
to a place with curtains and machines and needles
a place with men and women wearing white coats
carrying clipboards, wheeling computers, using strange
apparatuses
a place of beeps and charts and graphs
a place of no sleep
where I can hear the squish, squish, squishing sound
of liquid life coursing through my body
as I watch the jagged green pattern dancing across the
monitor
wondering what the steps mean

How do I trust my heart again
when there was no warning
and the pain wasn't so awful
but an urgency imposed
me with no preparation, not even a toothbrush
stripped and wearing the standard barely modest garb
such an ugly and odd uniform, really
but there I am
all wired up

right smack dab in the middle of the hustle and bustle
commenting that "drugs can be your friend" as I am
wheeled off
for a procedure I cannot even begin to wrap my head
around
before dawn has broken

And just in case they need access
they have shaved my private sacred mound
the slice of hair and hairlessness
perfectly symmetrical
like yin and yang without the yang
and I notice it resembles
one of those bakery black and white cookies
which amuses me
but not really

After much testing and retesting
after my heart has faded to 35% working order
they tell me that I am not in a risk category
that I do not fit a profile
and that I am experiencing,
in a word, "Takotsubo"
which means octopus trap in Japanese
and is a condition also known as Broken Heart Syndrome
a condition that women experience
due to stress

I understand
I know about broken hearts
I know about relationships that disappoint
and prove to be unworthy
I have paid the emotional price
more times than I care to remember

So after all this
how do I trust the heart again?
Dare I trust my heart again?

I thought not
until I experienced Takotsubo
and a man stepped forward
awakening love
opening my heart
so I could move on

The Walk

First touch before first kiss
good little parochial schoolgirl
new to menstruating
let alone wise to the ways of boys
instructed by my Irish Catholic mother
to walk the two miles to church
by myself
for Friday afternoon Lenten service

Perfect day for a walk
the sights so familiar
the curving road
pretty suburban houses
the smell of earth waking up
newly sprouted green grass
crocuses and daffodils stretching up
the breeze fresh

No one was around
occasionally a car would pass by
or my Mary Janes would crunch a pebble
otherwise all was quiet
and solitary
I was feeling independent

enjoying the reverie
of my own little girl thoughts

One sloping hill away from town
and the sanctuary of St. John's
a boy walked toward me
I did not know him
he was cute
I was shy
and did not look at him

He drew closer
and on approach
suddenly veered to my side of the walkway
reached out
cradled my crotch in his hands
murmured something I could not quite hear
and kept going

As if
as if
nothing was out of line
nothing was unusual
nothing was wrong

I kept going
not sure what had happened
not sure why my cheeks felt so hot

not sure why I felt ashamed
What had he said?
What was I to do?

So I kept walking
my feet did not stop
I did not look back
and never told a single soul

Secrets Weigh

Secrets exist
hidden within sly smiles
a pact
sealed with a kiss

But
there are terrible secrets
hanging in the air
secrets that weigh
dark moments not brought to the light of day

Gulped down and putrefied
a swallowed secret makes the victim gag
the burden of silence
worn like a mighty yoke
hurting the heart that bears it
extinguishing a fragment of soul

But make no mistake
women talk
in hushed and huddled whispers
and one day
the complicit solidarity
wrenches the chest open once more

And this is what lessens the load
of secrets that weigh

Kisses

Kisses, kisses on my nose
Kisses, kisses on my toes
Kisses morning, noon, and night
Kisses, kisses never bite

Plumage

Looking out the window
at the bird feeder
on a snowy winter's day
I comment on the brilliant red cardinal
and his mate, so demure
with muted plumage

I was informed
male birds are brighter
more ornate
to ward off predators
by deflecting attention away
from their dowdy female partners

I had never heard that theory before
so I studied avian life

I learned that males have vibrant plumage
as a signal to other guys
THIS is MY territory
And THIS is MY mate
best not to mess with me

And the splashy splay

of visual pomp
is…NO surprise…
an attempt to attract a female

Can't blame the cardinal
or peacock for that matter

For really
what male of any species
does not pose and preen
like James Dean
leaning against a car
pack of cigarettes
tucked recklessly in a T-shirt sleeve
toothpick wavering dangerously from lips

The only difference is
this postured demonstration
was in cardinal-red living color

I now see this desperate male pageantry in action
first hand
witness a man covering thinning grey hair
using pomade and cologne with abandon
wearing sharply tailored clothing
tugging lapels into place
before walking out the door

But his fancy is not feathered
and I know
he is neither a hunter nor a gatherer
and I would not place my trust in him
to protect the nest
if it was under attack

And so
I bide my time
and preen myself

Tossing Petals

Today was such a lovely day
the promising tease of early spring
the fresh beauty of the landscape
so green
it could scorch your eyes

I navigate back roads
fragrant with buds and blooms
the fields playgrounds for thoroughbreds
glistening coats shining in the sun
manes and tails flying banners
such wild, free energy
takes my breath away

I want it to take me away
I want to ride, keep riding, keep riding
faster and faster
until everything outside of me
becomes a dizzying blur
of swirling colors
with no up or down

I want to feel the intensity of air slapping my face
sweat and tears mingling midair

senses rendered senseless
until I lie
complete and exhausted
caressed by peace
as if encircled in the warmth of someone's arms

Will that ever happen again?

Hands on the wheel
my thoughts wander
down a long corridor
filled with lovers
each given his due
in the kaleidoscope
that is my memory

In my mind's eye
I can now see
how I picked a flower for each
always a daisy

plucking the petals
chanting
or maybe it was praying
"He loves me, he loves me not, he loves me..."
and, often,
it turns out that he did

Later
I would pick another daisy
for the man
breathe it in
then murmur
"I love you, I love you not, I love you, I love you not..."
because, quite often,
it turns out I did not

And I would toss the petals
into the wind
sigh
and wait for the arrival
of another spring

Today
I do not know if I will ever pick another daisy
perhaps I will

But right now
what I really want to do
is nick a bunch of lilacs from the cemetery
or bury my face in the sweet depth of a peony
and get drunk on the scent

Thoroughbreds

Thoroughbred women
with expensive hair, expensive teeth
manicured hands, pedicured feet
the privileged tan tossing their heads
price tags worn inside out
like leftover lottery confetti
condescend to others
who would clean up just fine
given half a chance

While their golf cart bronco boys
in saggy shorts and saddle shoes
display indistinct physiques
that wriggle in the sand trap
demonstrating no evidence
of rhythm and blues

But as for the displaced May Day photographer
snapping their pics
all that can be said is
no drunken jockey
is going to tame this filly
on the 18th hole

Music in the Fire Pit

Walking the grounds of the spiritual center
the fire pit at the lake
still, silent, abandoned
filled with ashes
cool, grey, weightless
evidence of prayer, purification, and release
a new white supplication
folded over, resting on top
scrawled with song and poetry
waiting for the next holy bonfire
the witnesses dancing salamanders
its fierce message demanding
"Do it now!"

What would you burn?

Photographs in the Attic

Ascending stairs
flights to dream memories
soft focus faces
black and white and filled with life
before etched with age
or too soon or too sudden partings
sweet still life memories
before goodbyes
or hands not held often or long enough
misty laughter
the eyes of love
captured
holding an essence
not faded like paper

The Ages of Arrowhead

In the river bed beach
along the muddy living waters
we search for pieces of time
not ours
to hold

Our heads bowed down
breaking the wind
listening to the gulls
our friends
tripping,
lightly laughing
over each new discovery

We find a pottery chip
a rusted knife
a carved stone
that builds to a perfect point

Sifting through sand
with hand, foot and eyes
we'll keep time
as we make our own
which is our standing still
until our pockets are full

The Birth of Rain

When rain was born
in the solar storm
hot from the belly of the rising sun
your thirst began to grow
and the new rain tasted like the cool, sweet, wet fruit
offered in the garden by the serpent who knows us by
name
fire-quenching paradise
coaxing and soaking life
from stilted, unanimated matter

I Don't Take it Personally

The cat
he loves to play with pens
especially the good ones
my favorite black Flairs in particular
fished out of pen holders or baskets
I find them tossed and scattered about on the floor
underneath rugs, furniture, and appliances
or sequestered in obscure corners
and so I reclaim them
to begin my writings once more

And when I'm not looking
sometimes the cat
shuts off the computer, too.
I don't take that personally, either

Things I've Learned

There are things I've learned
working with the musician
like what it means when a recording is "wet" or "dry"
holding and using a mic with voice and intent
listening deeply, separating sounds
to distinguish the high hat or the walking base
or the complex melody played by a waterfall

Then there are things I've learned by owning my first cat
like how a Hewlett Packard printer can fall a great distance
and still work
that Q-tips, pens, and other mundane things make the very
best toys
how what is closed can be opened and great heights can be
achieved
and the moods of whiskers and tail swishes

But my dog
oh my little dog
he teaches me all the time
what it means to be trusted and loved
how to show feelings in the moment and then let them go
and what it's like when your heart is delighted beyond
words

Solstice Song

Late December
the end of the year approaching
and the solstice is upon us
the rhythm of cycles continuing
as it has for ages
ancient as our bones

Collectively
we feel our blood flowing
with the dance of dark and light
the shortest day and longest night
known as the turning of the sun
or the sun standing still
at the Tropic of Capricorn
before reversing its direction.
How can we not feel its pull?

Outside in the dark stillness
of the brittle winter night
just the crunch of my boots on the snow
breaking the silence
I look up
engulfed by luminous vastness
I take a sharp breath

cold filling my lungs

Senses heightened
I am riveted
by a sound
far, far in the distance
breaking the silence
a sound
or rather a soft symphony
light, lilting
I can almost hum along
almost catch the tune
of the solstice song

Uptown Live

Musicians
lost in their own world
I am a voyeur
watching them dance
making love to sound
and to my soul

Sweaty, composed, ecstatic,
I feel their distant intimacy
wrapping notes around me
like hot confetti
they're wrapping notes around me
like hot confetti and cold, bracing rain
a wondrous living blanket
cloaking me
holding me in space

Sound waves of love sway
touch teasingly
tribal, pulsing, pushing
suddenly, gentle, slow, light
fingers graze
lips and tongue trill
heads bow, hips swing

always at one with instruments
and each other
inhaling, exhaling,
breathing into me

I got lost...

Haiku Flow

White ice confetti
Cascade of silent dancers
Soft celebration

Winter's wind song plays
Invisible melodies
Lacy green boughs dance

Spider web dances
Billows in hurricane gale
Delicate tremors

Dapple clouds paint sky
Glowing moon illuminates
Brush strokes of silver

Soft folds and shadows
Voluptuous mountain ridge
Seducing the sky

Train evangelist
Ranting about forgiveness
Singing subway hymns

Many blackbirds fly
Moving as one, in a heart
Swooping down to earth

Albino spider
White ghost dancing on mirror
Freezes in my gaze

Porcupine shaman
Hunched, wears quivering quill cape
Whispers prayers to leaves

Perfectly preserved
Bumblebee drunk in flower
What a way to go

Joint passed to the left
Oldest hippie in the world
Toking on wisdom

March 19

She sat
so still
so very still
in fact stiller than still
thinking if
if
if she was mad
wouldn't she be doing things
strange, strange things
things that made others stop and stare
as she pulled out her hair
sucking on fingers
a lunatic on the loose
racing around and around
chattering teeth
chattering words
silent screams shouted
at anyone passing by
anyone who would
or would not
listen

and all she could think about
all she could see

were the candles on the cake
flaming too high
so bright
blinding light
reaching
trying to put them out
she burned her hand
but did not make a sound
cradling scorched fist
her breath escaped
from drawn lips
and blew them out for her

and she sighed
counting them
knowing she was not mad after all
just another year older
if this was her birthday
if this day was March 19
if the cake was hers
sticking her fingers in the icing
licking them
licking them
licking them
until the sirens stopped shrieking
inside her head

The Study of Weather

This January sky has a certain brittleness
brilliant and ethereal
an almost unearthly silver light
the shimmery gauze curtain covering the sun
flattening the sky

Like any other animal, sniffing the wind
I feel the storm coming
as if it lives inside me
or is one of my own limbs

I like being in touch with Nature
I like knowing her subtle language
it has taken me a while to decipher it
to grasp the sensual nuances of her moods
child that I am of a legendary Manhattan suburb
the subject of Hollywood films and biting articles
a place where everything is white washed
everything homogenous
where status reigns
and houses and bank accounts are bigger than life
and the world is metered and measured in dollars and cents

Oh but I miss the beaches

the many moods of the salt water, waves and sand
swimming, floating, sailing
eating Cracker Jacks
flirting with lifeguards
scoring my first kiss

While there was chaos behind closed doors
I miss the sweet family moments
before death came too soon and tore it asunder
scattering my brother and sister and me like leaves on a
windy autumn day
mourning and lost for a while
to ourselves and each other
for at least a decade... or two....or three

But then the blood and memories
brought us together once more
and we now find ourselves
the generation riding atop the Ferris wheel
peaking as we see the descent
on a hot summer day

And today
with the raw wind howling at my heels
I realize I would not go back
I would not trade the study of weather
that organic sense of knowing
here and now

The Farmers Market Life

It's now the brilliant season
and so I imagine living a farmers market kind of life
one which so often eludes me
eyeing the perfection
of my new woven French market basket
found for a song at the thrift shop
I imagine drifting gracefully from booth to booth
hand picking perfect produce
for my evening table
filling my basket beyond full

I step outside and cut a bundle of peonies
this sunny June day
trying to decide between the white, pink, and burgundy
heavy headed they are
like ladies wearing layers of frilly petticoats
I decadently gather some of each
to arrange in the squat green metal vase
they look so lush and abundant
I go out and pick even more
to nestle among my austere bamboo stalks

Stepping back
I feel satisfied at last

the heady scent filling my cottage

Shutting out the world
I need to shut out the world
and I am thinking
this is the way to do it

Itchy for more sunshine
I drive to the new sacred garden site
after the party is over
to meander in solitude
along the stone paths
among the raised annual gardens
as the Zen rock waterfall
babbles soothingly
minding its own business
not questioning my motives
or asking anything of me

Turning into a different maze
I face the labyrinth
intricate with stone and brick circular paths
some patterns seem vaguely Moroccan
others like man-made best attempts at industrialized nature
in shades of slate and faded terracotta

Stepping deliberately
slowing my pace

slowing my breath
I know I cannot hurry to the center that awaits me
with the simple stone bench

It's about the trip not the destination as they say
listening to the chattering sunset birds
moving one step at a time
sequestered from the chaos of the outside world
cloistered from the hubbub
the exhausting useless energy
I find that prayer wells up easily
like another song chorus
I did not know I could sing
on this most brilliant day

In Venice I Could Sing

I really think I could sing
if I went to Venice
sing from my heart
amidst the lush colors and exotic landscape
imagining entanglements
with ripe embracing limbs
wanton exploration
of needless need
celebrating sensual pleasure
I just know I could sing
how could you not?

I wish I was there, as in *Summertime*
with Katharine Hepburn
braving foreign territory
embracing adventure
skirting the intimacy I desire
hiding behind the camera lens
I carry with me everywhere
hiding but watching
waiting to be unveiled
wanting to be wanted
waiting to unveil

Yes, singing could come easily
as naturally as breathing
that's how singing starts you know
among the bright colors of erotic longings
while pushing the boundaries of known existence
and floating, floating, floating
among ancient ruins and timeless landscapes
wrought iron, begonias, variegated coleus
colorful café umbrellas, tobacco, heady liquors
beguiling statues and leering gargoyles
lush and ripe with passion
alive with the promises of pleasure

I know I can sing…..
I am singing……

The Woman in My Belly

The woman in my belly
she aches for release
she gasps for freedom
breathing deep in soul
breathing deep in spirit
breathing in renewed life
renewed life for the birth of self

The woman in my belly radiates true essence
held by her firm hand, creative lions roar
raptors of power bow and move aside
barefoot she walks

She walks through the dark forest without fear of what
lurks in the bush
like a whisper
she glides along the path in a swirl of color
her white gown and veils trailing like mist behind her
they're trailing like mist behind her
and she leaves no shadow

She never forsakes herself

The woman in my belly loves wholly

gives freely
withholds nothing
eyes wide open she sees
she sees and receives
receives what is offered in rapture

Eyes wide open, she feels
no past, no future, encumber her vision
each moment alive, ever present
strung together like precious pearls
perfect prayers on a cosmic rosary
a cosmic rosary

Mary Magdalene

Mary Magdalene
gods and goddesses watched
they watched
as she pulled the sword out from her back
and held it up to the sky...

Excalibur...

from the deep recesses of flesh
that long denied a memory too hot to hold...
a memory that burned and scorched the waking cells
in her heart...
scorched the waking cells in her heart and in her brain...

and in the very depths of her soul
a memory of love that felt more like pain
the love felt like pain...
as she's learning to love herself
she's learning to love herself
she's loving herself now...

And the curve of her back
and the curve of her lips
and the curve of her hips and belly

as they rose and fell with the heat of her breath

They rose and fell on the night
when the clouds raced across the moon
to see which would collide with the horizon
clouds racing across the horizon
while Mary Magdalene combed her hair
and prepared the oil to wash her Beloved's feet

Pillow Book Tuesday

Pillow book says:
"When God made the first clay model of a human being
He painted the eyes, the lips, and the sex
He painted each person's name, lest they ever forget it
God approved of his creation
so He breathed the model to life, signing His own name"

Tuesday is no longer a pale day
forever now the color of pomegranate
passion's deepest sacred ripe red
reflected in the flame of an Archangel's candle
while we inscribe our pillow book
with murmurs and sighs and cries
winds howling and knocking outside
as potent as our love
God signing his name
next to ours

And So This Night

I am a loving phantom
a tender specter moving through the ethers
as haunting as an erotic breeze
silently passing through doorways
barefoot, drifting down dream hallways
in the peripheral vision of your heart
naked shadow by your side
holding with a whisper touch

Passion murmurs with imperceptible breath
soul to soul and skin to skin
sighing "Let me in...Let me in..."

I in Thee and Thou in Me

I'm the brightness in the light
The lucid dreamer in the night
You can feel me if you try
Beneath the skin is where I lie

I'm the soft voice in the dark
The warm blood beating in your heart
Listen close to hear my whisper
Like the beating of wings and wind on a river

I am oneness, above and below
The prayer that beckons you to follow

I'm the part that makes you whole
The energy that makes life flow
I'm the grace that went before
Leading to an open door

What you found I do not fear
What you love I too hold dear
What you seek I hope to find
What you are I have inside

You can feel me if you try

Beneath the skin is where I lie

Filling you beyond fullness
I in thee and thou in me…
Let me stir your soul

Apparently the Stranger Within

What do you do when the body is a traitor
like an uncaring stranger you thought you knew
who suddenly turns against you?
When you are uncomfortable in your own skin,
who do you turn to for solace and advice?
Even dreams seem like an enemy right now.

The other night the tone-deaf Swami
said to relax, relax, relax and let go
atonal chants sung with pure gusto.
My body cramping,
if I wasn't busy sinking into the abyss of blissful
nothingness
I would have laughed

Apparently life in an ashram isn't the answer
ascetic discipline isn't all it's cracked up to be
as Swami is seeking refuge in the freedom of getting a
Green Card
and living on his own with the help of the kindness
of strangers
not like my body

Swami said to subjugate wild thoughts

apparently subjugation leads to elimination,
I am seeking illumination
or at least going within in hopes of finding a glimmer
inside a body that's not behaving
a body that is not welcoming
like a sacred chamber
at least not right now.

Still, I love it

My Mother's Glamour

She wore makeup from the Five and Dime
Angel Face powder
"Soft, Soft Red" rouge powder blush
from a round pink tin decorated with a white bow
Helena Rubenstein lipstick

As she shopped for cosmetics
I perused the cluttered aisles
a wondrous sea of plastic bins
Wooly Willy with his metallic hair shards
colorful plastic horses
paddle balls
Ginny dolls
and amazing magic tricks

Influenced by Joan and Jane, Rita and Bette
the stoic Irish Catholic wife and mother
indulged in a bit of budget face paint
and on her dresser
displayed precious gifts
Emeraude Parfum and Chanel No. 5
rationed like war bonds
hardly used
but worshiped daily

And every night
she set her hair in pin curls
with bobby pins
covered by a hair net
but was modest
to a fault
used a bar of Ivory soap
to wash her face
saying that's all you need
in your beauty routine

She referred to her petite breasts
as kumquats
when I heard her say that
I did not even know what a kumquat was
or how sad a judgement
she made
diminishing herself

She smoked
a lot
had us kids walk up to Darby's
the neighborhood corner store
to buy her Raleigh unfiltered cigarettes
drank endless cups of coffee

as she smoked
coughed and gagged every morning

Little did we know
she was dying a slow, unglamorous death

Blood Dharma

Red
the color of blood and love
swirls its promise
from the bottom of the glass
sipped, slowly emptied,
I want to dive into its languid warmth
and drown

Grey
the brittle light of autumn
color of pale sky and mourning
leaves a taste neither bitter nor sweet
but salty with the sadness that comes
waking up to loss

The End of the World

I was very briefly
shown the end of the world
just a glimpse is all you need

It was flat and grey
with an odd filmy essence you could call celestial fog
that neither high beams nor low beams could penetrate
and it had no dimension whatsoever
just an expanse of nothingness
drifting, drifting
into more nothingness
apparently for all eternity
that is,
if the end can be considered an eternity

I, for one, am not sure
except I know what I have seen

For a long time
I have stopped watching the news
so over-stimulating
with its disturbing, graphic images
garish dancing banners
and the ceaseless yammering of well-coiffed talking heads

And now,
since my intimate vision of oblivion,
I have stopped reading it, too
except for the occasional headline
which is more than enough
to reaffirm
that we are a most vain, idiotic, and destructive species

And I am convinced
that when the planet has finally had
a bellyful of our nonsense
magnificent nature will carry on beautifully
and,
in her infinite wisdom,
unceremoniously dispose of us
as so much cosmic dust
to drift in the flat greyness
of nothingness

Estate Sale

Is this what it comes down to, the stuff of life?
Haphazard rubble strewn on tables, no semblance of order,
no sense of care
just remains and remnants for bargain hunters to sift
through
searching for the big cheap pay off
dusty collections no one really cares about

Thimbles and Hummels
chaotic stacks of books, thumbed-through volumes
Woodrow Wilson's autobiography, an outdated world atlas
decades of photos and sheet music
Christmas ornaments and jack-o-lanterns

The oddest of bedfellows in disarray
rusty tools and lopsided lampshades
amateur artwork and old greeting cards
bottles, vases, dishes, mugs
crocheted afghans and shabby pillows
cheap pocketbooks and costume jewelry
the musty scent of death

No reasonable offer refused!
Everything must go!

I open my wallet
hand two dollar bills to the cashier
and walk away with an empty scrapbook to fill

Throat of the Maiden

The predator
He hunts by night
a charismatic player
who knows how to win

As he enters the bar
the women eye him
lids fluttering with desire
ripe and ready for danger
it makes them feel more alive
and so they wait
losing themselves
in the depths of their wine

The stranger sidles up to the loveliest maiden
leans in, murmuring benign pleasantries
dripping with suggestion
she looks down
flashes a shy smile
and waits for the bait

Touching her elbow
he suggests a stroll
in the milky moonlight

then ushers her deftly out the door

Reaching the cobblestone alleyway
one arm swiftly engulfs her
the other grasps her trembling hands
both hearts beating wildly
the darkness swallows them

Winding himself around her body
the serpentine figure fuels her passion
she exhales
reveling to the thrill
of his cold touch

Tilting her head back
exposing her throat
his hungry lips and tongue
lap her pale skin
and she sighs
knowing what will come next

As he prepares to feast
she unfolds her wings
her nails sharpen and her lips retract
revealing massive fangs

Spinning around
she pins her male game against the wall

lays her cheek against his
breathes him in
then presses her lips against his
stifling his cries
and slowly, so slowly
sucks the life force out of him

It is so very, very easy
because men do not know
when a maiden offers her throat
it does not mean
he can freely feed

Gregorian Dessert

Her voice broke through
the restaurant clatter
clinking of glasses
forks raking plates
intimate mumbles
laughter
a sneeze...

Her voice broke through
the polite droning din
chairs scuffing tile
napkins unfurling
"God bless you"
the passing of cream...

The incantation of dessert specials
vibrated through the room
her undulating tongue
flicking saccharine syllables
"meringue...shaved and glazed....double-chocolat..."

A sugared Gregorian chant
awakening reverential ears

Modern Nocturne

(To be read with Harlem Nocturne melody playing in the background...)

Hold me closer this time
put your lips against mine
in the hot neon light
of a slick rainy night

We're beginning the dance
giving in to romance
know we're taking a chance
love won't hurt again

As your body draws near
I'm so ready to hear
all those words that you breathe
oh so soft in my ear

We continue to dance
giving in to romance
heartbeat calling your name
out again and again

Kiss me long, kiss me sweet
kiss me hot, kiss me deep
kiss me in the neon street
it's not time to say goodbye
Rain is falling…And so am I

Heartbeat calling your name
out again and again….
nocturne rain keeps falling…
And so am I, so am I…

Coldness

So bitter cold
trees are creaking
branches are wailing
at the end of his leash my little dog collapses on the blue
snow
picking him up, I curse the night sky
and rail against the weather gods

Inside now
I dive under the down blankets
cold and alone
ignore the wild banshee wind
knowing it will make me crazy
it's just a matter of time

This Winter

She is a cruel mistress, this winter
shrieking and slapping my face when I walk out the door
telling me she'll never release me into the warm arms of
another
while trysting with her bitter consort
the raging mountain wind
them laughing

I damn them for dominating me
shuddering and shivering
while they lash out repeatedly, relentlessly
taunting me to give up
collapse on the ground
freeze in their stare
and so I clutch my coat around my neck in defiance

This winter, she is impossible to court
nothing warms her frigid heart and lips
yet I am bound to her
and the more I try to embrace her
the harder I try to love her
she grows colder and more fierce
driving me away
driving me insane

but I am powerless to leave her grip

I need time, time, time
I need the caress of the sun on my face

Cooper Wind Dance

Cooper wind
cups my face
ripe autumn breath
cool pine needle perfume
while leaf headdress acrobats
bejeweled
in orange and yellow sequins
tumble and sway
before rustling,
nestling
into final destination
of decomposing
repose

My face
once turned skyward
now lost in the reflective mirage
transfixed
gazing
at the lake's shimmering glass mirror
of trees and sky
stroked by the waning red sun

My heart

longs to fly
with the leaf dancers
released,
at last,
to exhale
with the invisible
the unbridled winds
of Cooper Lake

Impossible Spring

Impossibly green
the only way to describe early spring
that one day
when everything suddenly comes to life
in the natural world
regardless of what is happening
in the unnatural world

Regardless of wars
or men tromping on other men
or men tromping on the environment
or another mass shooting
or more political double speak
or another self-serving political maneuver
or corporate swindle
or racial slur
or when no one admits the emperor has no clothes

But the green --
oh that green!
That impossible, blinding green
so fresh
so brash
so unrelenting

its scent so sublime
nature forging ahead
unstoppable, unfolding life
beyond reason
impossible, promising green
the fleeting color of hope
one day
one fine spring day
at a time

I Lie Still

Pablo Picasso invaded my interior scape
I have been disfigured
displaced eyes
fragmented breasts
chest torn asunder
heart wrest open, ready to burst
feelings fractured
refracted
like a shattered mirror

When did Salvador Dali take his brush to my eye sockets
stroking them into salty dripping rivets
placing the face of the watch into my mouth
elongating the seconds
extending my pain

Jackson Pollack spewed emotions up and down my spine
haphazard attack
the paint still wet
finger-painted anxiety
smeared upon my belly

How brittle am I?
I lie still

tremble
holding my breath
waiting for Michelangelo to rescue me
caress me
coax me out from the stone
before I shatter

The Last Embrace

The moment death embraces
with complete, consuming love
the release, the freedom
as the world shifts into particles
the glaze, the liberation
as the world shifts into particles

Particles of sound
and waves and colorless shapes
shifting from fragments of what was
to the new reality
that always will be

Oh the light
how it burns and beckons you to be one
with all that is
and with all that you are
as death envelops
with its warm embrace of love

But it is the dark moments before I fear
that send me racing to and fro
to clutch and grab at life
that is but a whispering shadow of home…

I run from feeling snuffed

This meager candle
that is really a flame
a pulsing, piercing, shattering light
blinding, unblinking brightness
unashamed of its power

Behold your power
a thousand candles bow to you
but yet you look away
unable to bear your own brilliance

What is this eternal tie?
I cannot see
but it lies in wait
so silent
so calm
I feel it as close as a brush with the wind...
It's like the wind...

When death bestows its final embrace
how I ache
how I cower and bow
how I desire and withdraw
look...
Do not look...
Look...

Do not look…
Wait…Wait…
Like a patient lover it knows

I must cross alone
Oh, but to embrace you when death comes
I will feel no fear

I embrace you without fear

A thousand candles bow to you
A thousand candles bow to you
A thousand candles

Vision

Don't close your eyes
don't turn away
it's what you can't see
that gets in the way

The blindness it lulls
as it puts you to sleep
shuts out the pain
thoughts can't run too deep

Pretend it's not there
pretend it's not there
because if you look
you might have to care

Scoundrels seek apathy
a stupor-like state
that keeps you in line
so you won't deviate
from numbing normality
the middle of the road
once you think for yourself
life's a heavier load

You'll see the injustice
you'll feel all the pain
you'll hear all the madness
and feel all the shame

Pretend it's not there
pretend it's not there
because if you look
you might have to care

Ask them no questions
they'll still tell you lies
all prettied up
in sweet-smelling disguise

You pick up the blindfold
you wear readily
so you won't have to look
and don't have to see

Pretend it's not there
pretend it's not there
because if you look
you might have to care

When truth looks squarely
right into your eyes
it glares, it shatters,

it makes you cry
so many wounds begging
to be healed
so many realities
waiting to be revealed

And then...
you'll see the injustice
you'll feel all the pain
you'll hear all the madness
and feel all the shame

Release the blinders
untie the cord
vision is power
and truth is the sword
change begins
with a sweeping view
so open your eyes—
it starts with you

Don't close your eyes
don't turn away
it's what you can't see
that gets in the way

Skin on Poppies

Black, white, yellow, bronze, brick
skin on poppies
we all bleed the same
like the flowers in Flanders Field

Eyes blink
seeing or not
lips curl
in smile or snarl
Noses discern
scent and intent
heads twist and turn
thoughts provoke

We inhale, we exhale
gasp in joy, in ecstasy
in sorrow, in pain
sighs escape like mist
and dreams
conceived in womb of night
burn bright

Fingers seek hands seek skin seek touch
seek comfort seek desire seek pleasure

seek heat seek love seek oneness

Color is misleading
it can turn on you
seen in a false mirror
reflecting the illusion of otherness
perpetuating a rift in unity
undermining the dignity of humanity

Despite our sheath
despite our fragile skin
in our heart of hearts and soul of soul
we all want
we all need
we all bleed the same
poppy red

Blood and Ink: Solders' Letters Home from War

(Revolutionary through Contemporary)

I.

Dear Folks
Mommie and Dad
Pa
Dearest Mother
Beloved Wife
Sweetheart Mine
My Precious

I am still in the land of the living
all the gang are writing post-mortem letters
and kind of half ashamed of themselves for doing it

It is a strange feeling to me
but a very real one
that every letter I write home to you
may be the last that I shall write
or you read

I don't know why I am writing this

I really hope that this letter never gets to you
because if it does that means I am dead

I write
for you will be sure to hear
that I was killed in the fight last Sunday
for it was reported that I was
but I write this with my own hand
to testify
that I am yet in the land of the living

It is pretty hard to check out this way
without a fighting chance
but we can't live forever
I'm not afraid to die
I just hate the thought of not seeing you again

I do not want you to think I am depressed
indeed on the contrary
I am very cheerful
but out here
in odd moments
the realization comes to me
of how close death is to us

It seems like a dream more than anything else

II.

They have been teaching us bayonet fighting
it makes your arms ache
when you lunge at an imaginary enemy
the rifle at arm's length
with this hard training
they will either make a man of me
or kill me
you ought to see me in my shrapnel helmet and gas mask
it would make you laugh

Here I am,
20 years old now
I'm a man now
not a teenager anymore

I recently saw some of the dead boys they had taken off
the battlefield
if some of the men back home
whom of personal ambition attempt to prolong the war
could see them
I'm sure the war would soon end

When you look at them you can't help but think
why are they dead
I hope these men have not given their lives for
empty words

You know how they say
war is not like the movies show it
well, they're wrong
it's exactly like the movies.

III.

Such a storm of balls
I never conceived possible for men to live through
shot and shell shrieking and crashing
canister and bullets whistling
hissing most fiend-like through the air
until you could almost see them.

Oh Lord
if ever a fellow was afraid
absolutely frightened to death
it was this child

A rattle of musketry
at first like pattering drops upon a roof
then a roll, crash, roar, and rush
like a mighty ocean billow upon the shore
chafing the pebbles
wave on wave
with deep and heavy explosions
like the crashing of the thunderbolts

How close death is to us
soldiers love a general that loves and tries not to lose them

I shall never forget that battle
my company suffered most
there are only four of us left out of 100
I consider myself lucky getting off with wounds

Today is probably the worst day
I have ever lived in my entire short life
my best friend in this shithole was killed
he was only 22 years old
I feel that if I was only half second sooner
in pulling the trigger
he would still be alive
strange how short a time half a second is
the difference between life and death

All the bodies had disappeared
into the water
there was nothing left but blood
and an empty raft
swarms of sharks were everywhere
the sharks ate well today
later darkness descended and the rains came

The third shell struck and killed my horse

bursting
blew him to pieces
knocked me down
and tore off my right arm

One may get used to rifle bullets
and does
but you can never get used to the shells
they make such an awful noise

The truth is
when bullets are whacking against tree trunks
and solid shot are cracking skulls like eggshells
the consuming passion in the breast of the average man
is to get out of the way

IV.

In less than one minute
a relatively peaceful day went straight to hell
after you've been here
only as short a time as I have
your ideas change

If there is a place called Hell
this surely must be it
we must be the Devil's disciples
doing all his dirty work

I keep asking myself if there is a God
then how the hell come young men
with so much to live for
have to die

Perhaps you would like to know
the spirit of the men out here now
the truth is
every man is fed up
almost past bearing
not a single one has an ounce of what we call patriotism
left in him

All that every man desires now
is to get done with it and go home
the greatest hope of a great majority
is that rioting and revolt at home
will force the government to pack in on any terms

V.

No big thing
but I finally got to take a shower after a week
boy did I stink
the dirt must have been ¼" thick

I need a fountain pen

I need a wrist watch of the shock proof variety
both my fountain pen and wrist watch are broken
I also need a sleeveless woolen khaki-colored sweater

I received your parcel
the pineapple was delicious
the banana was crushed but I ate it just the same

Yesterday was Thanksgiving
most of the doughboys had turkey
it's amazing when you think of all of us
so far from home
observing still
in the midst of a battlefield
Thanksgiving

I think that we shall see a fight soon
I know not where I shall be when I write next

We have two secession spies here in camp
and a nigger that knows where there is a lot of guns
wagons
mules
and other things
he says that he will tell me where they are
if I go with him and take some men with me

I have flown 1,500 hours now

and in those hours
I could tell you a lifetime story
Today I am 21
far away but coming home older
I dream of her hand touching mine
telling me to come home
but I wake up
and it's some sergeant telling me I have to fly

He got his death wound
when fighting desperately side by side with me
in the wildest hand grenade and machine-gun fight man
could live or die in
I am said to have absolutely no nerves
I saw over a hundred of our men blown to fragments
by a big shell about 200 yards from where I was lying
It's turned midnight and I think I will sleep now

VI.

If we never meet on this earth
I hope we will meet in Heaven
where partings will be no more

When this reaches you
for me there will be no more war
only eternal peace and waiting for you

Au revoir my own sweetheart
God will keep you safe till the storm's over
I really did love you with all I had
you were everything to me

I won't live till morning
so goodbye my friends
may God be with you all
goodbye
God bless my poor soul

Golden Tongue

If I had a golden tongue
words would swoon
licking you into ecstasy
delighting with metallic pleasure.
Truth would be precious.

Place a ruby in my mouth and listen.
It speaks tales of languid passion.
The essence of bitten emerald fragments
trail from my lips
leaving the exquisite taste of freedom.
I laugh, swallowing sapphires
that shake you to the bone.

And from the depths of my soul
diamonds radiate more wisdom
than we could possibly comprehend
in many, many lifetimes.

White hot metal, cool hard compounds
co-existing in unified, molten perfection
spilling over as I open my mouth

What is Sweet, What is Good

Now is the time to recall what is sweet, what is good
in the face of darkening days
in the face of facts and exaggerations
in the face of fear and fear mongering
that is relentlessly in our face

We need to pause, to tune out, to turn away
and just breathe quietly
letting peace sink in
at least for a while
to just take that moment to moment
moment

We need to recall and call upon what is sweet, what
is good
simple pleasures that give us joy
like a bed made with freshly laundered sheets
stirring a fragrant soup simmering on the stove
watching the bouncing prance of a happy dog
picking up a cat that reaches up to be hugged
hearing a good friend's voice over the phone
feeling the brisk spring wind softly slap your face alive
noticing the first new buds are on a venerable old tree
catching a glimpse of the golden glow of sunlight at those

certain hours
receiving the texted photo of the new baby born
amidst chaos
looking for all the world like Buddha

Focusing on what is sweet, what is good
to make you feel so alive, at this moment

Hymn

Love him
Love her
Love Hymn
Lover

About the Author

Patricia Mason-Martin is an author, poet, performer/actor, and freelance writer/communications professional who has been featured at numerous venues, festivals, on the radio, and published in various periodicals and anthologies. A member of the Author's Guild, she is author of six books, and recorded a spoken word and music CD with composer producer/musician Gus Mancini. www.patriciamartin.com